AMBLESIDE REMEMBERED
'People and places, past and present'

By Rose Steele

Compiled by Anne Bonney

Dedicated to my family, friends and Amblesidians

Published by Helm Press
10 Abbey Gardens, Natland, Kendal, Cumbria LA9 7SP
Tel: 015395 61321

First published 2001

Typeset in Electra 10pt & 9pt

ISBN 0 9531836 8 8

Typeset and printed by
Miller Turner Printers
The Sidings
Beezon Fields
Kendal
Cumbria LA9 6BL

Front cover: Photograph by Lowe of Patterdale of Lake Road
Back cover: Photograph by Stengel of Salutation Hotel, Market Place about 1900

CONTENTS

Rose Steele

INTRODUCTION

My family, was called Gregg and were originally quarrymen in Cumberland. My father lived at Torver before marrying my mother and settling at 3 Smithy Brow, Ambleside, where I was born in 1935. I attended the local junior and senior girls' schools, before getting my first job as an office junior at Gatey and Heelis Solicitors in the town.

I then worked for a few years in Kendal before marrying my husband, Raymond. We emigrated to Africa for eighteen years before coming back to Kendal in 1979 and settling with our two daughters, Wendy and Valerie.

I started collecting old post cards of Ambleside as a hobby fifteen years ago and now have a large collection, to which I am still adding. I decided to put some of these photographs into a book, so that they could be shared with others with a similar love and interest in Ambleside.

In compiling this book I have engaged the help of a friend, Anne Bonney, who has assisted in the research and compilation of this work, together with the invaluable help and advice of John Marsh. I would also like to thank in particular, my sister, Irene who has lived in and around Ambleside all her life, together with her husband. Also to friends and Amblesidians who have lent photographs and given generously of their time.

I discovered a great deal when I started researching the story behind the photographs. The Lake District has acted since the eighteenth century as a kind of magnet for poets, painters, authors, educationalist and philosophers alike. They told, painted or wrote of the beauty of the Lake District and this in turn generated an interest countrywide. People, mainly the wealthy came to start with and bought plots of land and built their mansions. Later when travel improved and we had rail as far as Windermere, it became more accessible to a greater part of the population.

I have tried to give as much information as possible to give the reader a flavour of these times and where I have thought useful or beneficial I have side-stepped slightly to give a little more information on the person(s) who has lived there, high-lighting their impact in the development of Ambleside. This book is filled mainly with old photographs and tales of the past, so forgive me for having transgressed on to some living people who I think are worthy of note. I leave you to find them and trust you will whole heartedly agree with their inclusion.

My collection, beginning with my earliest photograph, spans nearly a century, through the mid-nineteenth to the middle of the twentieth century and has been gleaned from many sources. The ancient town of Ambleside is shown as it was then in photographs by previous generations of its inhabitants and early visitors to the Lakes.

Whilst every effort has been made to trace all copyright holders, I apologise to any holders I have not acknowledged and would be grateful if I could be notified of any correction to be incorporated in any future edition. I have also tried to make it as accurate as possible, so please forgive me if I have made any slight errors along the way.

I hope you will enjoy your trip back through time as you turn the pages.

Rose Steele
Spring 2001

Ambleside taken in the mid 19th century in the early years of photography when St Anne's Church was the village church

CHAPTER ONE
WATERHEAD

The Great Freeze of 1894-95 when lake after lake froze, until even Windermere was one thick
sheet of ice. A number of gales had swept Britain during the autumn, culminating in one called
the Great Storm. This was then followed by seven weeks of hard frosts, which lasted into March.
The main spell was between 5th and 13th January when the lake froze hard (nine inches thick).
There were short thaws followed quickly by hard frosts.

The lake took on a carnival atmosphere with bands playing and people skating to the music.
Others walked, sledged, played curling, ate, drank and generally enjoyed themselves.
Thousands travelled to Lakeland from all over the country. Mid-week excursion trains from
Liverpool, Manchester and Lancaster were packed. Hotels and boarding houses were full. It was
a joyous time, even the police were on ice – they formed an ice patrol! People came and went
daily – estimated numbers ranging from three to eight thousand arriving and departing.

Then, sadly for some it came to an end and everything reverted back to normal – but what a
good time they'd all had. This picture shows some of them on the lake at Waterhead, obviously
watching the camera man who was taking their photograph.

(Photo: Hayes Garden World)

Brown's of Ambleside were a famous coaching firm from horse days into motor bus days. Here one of their coaches is seen at Waterhead, near the Wateredge Hotel, in the early 1900s setting off for a day trip from the hotel.

Note of interest

Brown's coaches used to have a tin shed up Nook Lane, Ambleside (below the slaughter house) where they kept the old horse-drawn coaches, when they were no longer used. I remember we used to sneak in as children between the metal sheets on the side of the shed and play on them. They were lovely!

Another photograph taken of the Wateredge Hotel in the 1920s by Edward Sankey of Barrow. The age of the motor car is about to begin.

The Waterhead Hotel started life as a small establishment, which was improved and enlarged over the years. It is seen here in its nearly modern state in a photograph by Matthews of Bradford in the 1920s.

Cows standing taking their ease in Lake Windermere, looking across to Waterhead in the 1930s.

'The Grange' was a delightful Georgian mansion at Waterhead, which in its later life became 'The Romney Hotel'. In this early twentieth century photograph it is seen as 'The Grange Private Hotel.'

The alterations that converted the original house into the three-storey 'Romney Hotel' are easy to see in this later photograph. The hotel has now been replaced a few years ago by luxury flats and is now called 'Romney Grange'.

The holiday season at Waterhead is clearly seen by these 1920s photographs.

Above, a Matthews of Bradford picture shows 'The Swan' at the Waterhead Pier. The picture shows the first lake steamer of that name which was scrapped in the 1930s.

Below, Sankey's picture shows an array of different types of motor transport, which had by then replaced the horses and had carried on the business through the nineteenth century. Note in the right of the foreground there is still one horse and cart.

The lake has always been treated as a highway (and legally so) and there has been some kind of boat service since the late 1700s. In 1836 a regular arrangement was made between James Gibson of Ambleside and a Mr White of Newby Bridge for a large rowing boat to leave each end and meet at Ferry Inn. A horn was blown in Ambleside before Mr Gibson set off.

The Birdhouse Mouth at the 'Three Foot Brandeth', where the Rothay and Brathay join and become one river, was the ancient and customary place for boats to be kept, but the Waterhead landing place must have been started when steamers began. The 'Lady of the Lake' began to ply in 1845 – this was a wooden paddle steamer.

From a much earlier period at the beginning of the twentieth century comes this photograph by Raphael Tuck & Sons of the scene at the Waterhead Steamer Pier. Note the two hotel horse buses on the right. The Esplanade had yet to be developed by the row of big hotels and boarding houses that later became Ambleside's spacious Youth Hostel.

The Toll Bar at Waterhead was just on the Windermere Road from Waterhead Pier and was part of the turnpike road system that ceased to exist in 1887, when the county's roads were taken over by the Quarter Sessions which ran the County in these days before the County Council. This is an early photograph by the famous Ambleside photographer Herbert Bell of Lake Road, Ambleside. *(Photo: John Marsh Collection)*

The Roman Fort, Galava, at Ambleside became in the years before the First World War, the site of the Officers Training Corps Annual Camp, where university boys were trained, unaware of the horrors to come from which many did not return. Here is the 1909 camp seen across the River Rothay. *(Photo: John Marsh Collection)*

This lovely photograph of a little boy and girl dressed in rather over large hats – Mary and Edmund Troughton from Gas Works Cottage – all dressed up for an Ambleside event about 1910 – outside Ambleside Boys' School. Note the dress of the boys behind and the heavy boots – I wonder if they were made locally?

(Photo: John Marsh Collection)

CHAPTER TWO
LAKE ROAD (SOUTH)

Wansfell Tower Hotel under the ownership of the Dixon's in the early part of the twentieth century. The building has since been converted into flats.

This photograph by Lowe of Patterdale shows delivery boys having 'a chat' out of sight of their boss. The Lake Road fountain can just be seen on the right.

Above: Fisherbeck Hotel, Ambleside in the 1930s, with the car park to the right. I remember when the fair was in the car park and extended into Lanty's field (named after the farmer who had Fisherbeck Farm) and they knocked the wall down to enter the field. The hotel and car park are still here today.

Left: Low Fold, Lake Road, Ambleside about 1906. On the reverse of the card reads: - "Low Fold, where we stayed in Ambleside, with our hostess standing at the door. The road from Windermere to Ambleside runs past the door; but we had an unobstructed view from our second storey window across the meadow beyond, to the hills and scar and the Rothay river and the head of Lake Windermere that was perfectly charming." (This was prior to the Alpine Gardens mentioned on the next photograph which replaced the meadow).

The Hayes Family

Thomas Richard Hayes and his family first came to Ambleside in the beginning of the nineteenth century from Staveley, together with his family of four sons and a daughter. They set up a nursery at Mill Row. Later they opened a Seedsman Shop on Smithy Brow and then a larger nursery at Rydal Road (this closed on the death of the last surviving brother in 1876).

The oldest grandson of Thomas Richard, (also of that name) began a nursery in Grasmere opposite the church. They too had a family of five. One of their sons, also a Thomas Richard, wanted a more formal study of horticulture and went as a student to the Royal Nurseries in Birmingham, later to Belgium, France and Germany to study the rare alpine flowers in the meadows of Switzerland and France. His knowledge was to prove immeasurable in laying the foundations to the T.R. Hayes & Sons we know today.

In 1890 he returned and opened nurseries in Keswick. He developed the much, acclaimed Alpine Gardens between the town and the lake. He had a flair for landscaping – particularly creating rock gardens using Westmorland water worn limestone. He exhibited at Chelsea and created the precedent that has been followed by future generations of exhibitors.

With his hard work and success under his belt, he decided in 1908 to turn again to Ambleside and re-establish the family name, by buying a piece of land called 'Peggy Parrock', near Waterhead, in readiness for his sons. Fortunately, his three sons were all interested in gardening. Reg went into agriculture and the Colonial Service. Richard, the oldest, went to Art College at Stratford and then to Christchurch to study alpines before going on to Kew Gardens in London. After the First World War he returned to the Keswick Nurseries to join his father and Geoffrey in developing the Ambleside Nursery. The three won many prizes with their landscaping, using rock and water gardens and gained many large contracts i.e. Dutch Gardens at Sizergh Castle, as well as many public works and parks.

This is an early 1920s advertising card for T R Hayes & Sons, Alpine Gardens, Ambleside.

The Keswick Nurseries closed after the death of their father and the family concentrated on Ambleside. Richard had three sons, Geoffrey the oldest, Peter Richard and Thomas Leith. Richard left his nurseries to join the War. The nurseries were turned to producing much needed food during the Second World War and many of the plants were lost. Richard and Geoffrey had to re-establish the nursery once again in 1946. Geoffrey decided 'to go it alone' and purchased the Grasmere Nursery that was once his great uncles'. Richard continued with the Ambleside Nursery and was joined by his two sons.

Richard died in 1960 and Geoffrey in 1978. In 1988 Peter went to Scotland to set up a nursery whilst Leith continued in Ambleside. We leave the 6th generation Hayes to move onto the 7th generation, with Michael Richard and Thomas Richard who bring us into the twenty-first century. Leith died in 1992 and his widow Elizabeth carries on the nursery today, together with her son Richard (Thomas Richard). Michael Richard went to join Peter in the nursery in Scotland. The nursery has changed much from its humble beginnings to the multi-million pound Hayes Garden World we have today. Nowadays it is spread sizably over seven acres and sells plants, flowers, shrubs, garden furniture, in fact everything you need for the garden, plus as many gardening services as any one could wish for and is surely one of the best in the country to which their forebears would have been rightly proud!

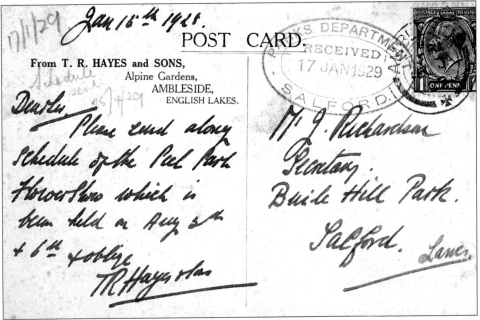

Reverse of the card pictured on previous page.

Geoffrey Hayes (1897-1978) photographed here by G P Abraham of Keswick
(Photo: Hayes Garden World)

The log cabin that was brought over from Norway in 1905 by the famous artist, Alfred Heaton Cooper as his very first studio and was reassembled in the garden of Dr Mandle's Restaurant, behind the Crown Hotel, in Coniston.

Annoyingly it cost him more shipping it over and transporting it to the Lakes, than the actual building cost. Later the cabin was moved to the corner of Lake Road and Wansfell Road, Ambleside. It stood there for many years until the rent became too excessive and a plot of land was purchased at Fisherbeck, where it still stands today. This rare picture by Herbert Bell shows the building on its original site in Coniston. Below, this up-to-date picture shows where it stands today and was taken by Anne Bonney.

Alfred Heaton Cooper
(1863 – 1929)

Born in Manchester and the oldest of six children. His father and mother worked in the mills in Bolton. His father was an accountant. On leaving school Alfred also went to train as an accountant at Bolton Town Hall. This did not last however, his love of art shone through and he gained a scholarship, which enabled him, in 1884, to go to the Westminster School of Art in London. Alfred was much influenced by artists like Turner and Constable.

After his training, Alfred travelled abroad for a while, before staying in Scotland and the Lake District. He spent a year in Norway where he met and married a local girl but found he could not make a living, so he returned to England. He came back to Bolton for a time, then Southport, before finally coming back to settle in the Lake District. Times were hard and especially so for an artist. Their luck changed when one day he was asked to illustrate a book for Blacks, the publishers. It was around this time that he purchased and shipped over the log cabin for his studio but decided that it would be better sited at Ambleside, so it was moved once again.

His whole life revolved around

Alfred Heaton Cooper, at Coniston in 1906 standing with paint brush in hand at his easel
(Photo: Heaton Cooper Studio)

painting and his wife and family. His wife Mathilde ran the studio, when he was out on the fells painting the scenes he so loved. Alfred was commissioned again on a number of occasions by Blacks to illustrate their guide books and he also exhibited works, in both water colour and oils regularly in the Royal Academy.

Alfred and Mathilde had two daughters and three sons, sadly one the sons died a few months old from pneumonia. The studio today is still owned and run by the family.

Alfred was well liked and respected by all who knew him. His paintings today are well known and many are sold as prints from the Heaton Cooper Studio in Grasmere. Tourists from all over the world visit the studio and come away with a memento to remind them of their visit and this talented local artist.

Langdale and Ambleside Mountain Rescue Team. Seen here during a practise session on Tongue Ghyll, above Grasmere, in 1969-70. Left to right: Peter Bell, Chris Lewis, Dave Mounsey, Paddy Daley, Malcolm Crossley, Andrew Flitters, Ron Black,   ?, Mark Osmond and Richard Goodson.

(Photo: Langdale and Ambleside Mountain Rescue Team)

Langdale and Ambleside Mountain Rescue Team

Today the team have a Rescue Centre in Lake Road. They will inevitably be called out to attend some emergency whereby a walker has got into difficulties, lost or injured on the fells. This was a far cry from the early days of mountain rescue when St John's Ambulance used to attend. Coniston had the earliest team in this area in the 1900s, followed by Langdale, when climbing became more popular up Dungeon Ghyll. In the 1950s we hear stories of Syd Cross, of the Dungeon Ghyll Hotel, who was an excellent climber, responding to the call, and readily accepting the challenge and taking any able, willing volunteers who happened to be in the bar to assist and become stretcher-bearers if necessary.

Times have moved on, though the needs seem to be greater than ever. One name that comes to the fore, as being synonymous with mountain rescue in Ambleside, is Stewart Hulse. He first came to the Lake District in 1969 as an experienced St John's Ambulance Volunteer. His interests in this together with his love of the fells led to the formation of the Ambleside Fell Rescue Team. His house was used as a temporary rescue base and then in 1969-70 the team amalgamated with Langdale Mountain Rescue Team and a dedicated base was purchased. Stewart was first made an assistant team leader in 1982 and then team leader in 1987. The team has forty-five volunteers, made up of men and women and on average is called-out more than eighty times a year. Usually between fifteen to twenty-five members of the team turn out at any one time. In 1974 the team initiated the joint help of the RAF helicopter, which was a giant leap forward from these early days. The RAF helicopter usually comes from Bulmar and uses the Rugby Club pitch at Galava Park to land. Today this highly trained and motivated volunteer group, who rely on public donations for funding, is highly organized and kitted out with the latest technology that it can afford, together with four-wheel drive vehicles, communication and medical equipment – to rush to the aid of any hill walker or climber in trouble. This is a dedicated service, provided by a team that is worthy of countrywide recognition and is second to none, for which we are justly proud.

Stewart Hulse taken in the mid 1990s with Tony Richards in the background.
(Photo: Langdale and Ambleside Mountain Rescue Team)

Mountain Rescue Team receiving a generous gift of tyres from a tyre company, pictured here in mid 1970s at the Base before it was modified. Left to right: Ian Wall, Norman Walker, Brian Morgan, Tyre Sponsor, Carl Wright, Tony Richards, Stewart Hulse, brothers – Paul and Martin Cornforth.

(Photo: Langdale and Ambleside Mountain Rescue Team)

The team pictured at Ambleside Cricket Club in the 1980s

Front row, left to right: John Gaskell, Maureen Penman, Richard Goodson, Dr Earnshaw, Norman MacVeigh, Joy Grindrod, John Graham, Gordon Spragg, Malcolm Grindrod, Brian Marshall, Martin Scrowston and Paul Allonby (photographer). (Plus Rescue Dogs).

Middle row, left to right: Stewart Hulse, Colin Earnshaw,   , Andrew Flitters, Peter Bell, Earnie Thompson, Bev Yates, Peter Natrass, Dave Owen and Ian Williams.

Back row, left to right: Jim Fuller, Dave Till, Dr Alan Jackson, Peter McDonald, Carl Wright, Peter Farrand, Peter Ennis, Simon Fahy, Brian Morgan, Peter Monaghan, Dr Bowen (standing with door open).

                                                                    (*Photo: Paul Allonby*)

ESTABLISHED 1781

Memo. from

JAMES BENSON,

Black & Whitesmith, Fitter, Turner, & Machinist

POSTAL ADDRESS:
"FISHER BANK,"
AMBLESIDE.

SHOEING FORGE,

Ambleside, _Augt 5th_ 19 11

To _Messrs The Exos late James Benson._

Gentlemen

I shall thank you for acknowledgement,
of recit of my previous letter.
it will suffice.

Thanking you in anticipation

Yours Obediently

Wm Jas Benson

19 A Westmorland Carter.

Left: A Westmorland Carter. This was
one of the people who delivered goods by
horse and cart and would need the services of the blacksmith.

Ian Benson

Ambleside's last blacksmith who retired a few years ago as a result of ill health. His family have been blacksmiths at 'The High Shop', on Blue Hill, Ambleside for over two hundred years. The blacksmith's was well situated for trade, as the old Roman road passed by the door and horseback riders and horse-drawn coaches would climb steadily to Wansfell and across to Kirkstone.

The business was started by Ian's great, great, great-grandfather, Harry Benson in 1781, when the main business would be shoeing horses and wheel-hooping. The work they have done over the years has changed to accommodate the requirements of the time. However, much of the old traditional equipment was still in use until Ian sadly closed the doors for the last time. They had two original hand-operated bellows that breathed life into the old forge to enable iron bars to be moulded into shape. Ian still had many of the old tools and anvils, including a hooping-plate for making coach and cartwheels and the machine for bending the hoops. Ian, (the only son), took over from his father Edward Jackson Benson, known affectionately as 'Teddy', after serving a ten year apprenticeship at George Reed's, at the Victoria Forge, in Windermere. His father had moved away from shoeing horses to making wrought iron gates, bannisters and standard lamps for customers. Ian continued in the same vein, including making complicated fire escapes and spiral staircases.

'Teddy' Benson at work in 1967 in his Ambleside Smithy, with the hand-powered bellowed forge behind.

(Photo: Ian Benson)

Ian Benson at work in the smithy in 1981.

(Photo: Ian Benson)

The rough dirt Lake Road lined with trees which are now long gone. The roads were dusty in summer and wet and muddy in winter – before the days of tarmacadam! The large houses on the left are now guesthouses providing accommodation for the many visitors.

The bottom picture shows a 1930s scene with Atkinson's exclusive ladies and men's wear shop on the left-hand side, which is still in business today. Lambs Temperance Private Hotel opposite with an array of holiday hat wear on display is shown on the right.

CHAPTER THREE

ST ANNE'S CHURCH
AND SMITHY BROW

Old Church, Ambleside.

The oldest part of Ambleside is that surrounding the site of St Anne's Church. The history of Ambleside's Old Church, as the mountain chapelry of St Anne is obscure, though we know it was in existence in 1597. First records commenced with a Christening in 1642, burials from 1675 and weddings in 1680. The chapel was situated north of the stock or 'Above Stock' and was therefore classed as being in Grasmere Parish, so the townsfolk had to be carried along Nook Lane and along the old 'Corpse Road' to Grasmere for burial. The present church we see here in this early nineteenth century Stengel of London photograph replaced the old church in 1812.

I remember the Youth Club meeting here, as well as attending dances. This ancient church like so many others has been transformed into flats in recent years.

How head, where this couple are standing with their cat in the doorway, is situated next to St Anne's Church. This is one of the oldest houses remaining in Ambleside, incorporating stone from the old Roman Fort and river cobbles, with some parts dating back to the sixteenth century. These houses would previously have been made of wood and thatch. The large rounded chimneys, deep porches and doorways and the original mullioned windows are still here today and some are now holiday cottages.

Right: A young lady walking down the middle of Smithy Brow (once known as Golden Rule Hill) towards Rydal Road on a winter's day, just passing the Golden Rule Inn in the early 1900s.

Left: Lowe of Patterdale took many photographs of the Lake District of which this must be the oddest as it only shows the yard at the back of the Golden Rule Inn. The front of the Inn opens onto Smithy Brow.
(Photo: John Marsh Collection)

GOLDEN RULE INN, AMBLESIDE

THE GOLDEN RULE INN

DO TO OTHERS AS YOU WOULD BE DONE BY

Right: This is an early postcard of the sign that originally hung outside the 'Golden Rule Inn'. This was reproduced onto postcards that were for sale in the Inn for locals and tourists alike. The golden rule being 'Do to others as you would be done by!'

1 Smithy Brow, Ambleside.

A later picture showing springtime in Smithy Brow in the early 1930s, shows Swaledale sheep and lambs returning to their heaf on the fells after lambing. (Heaf is the term given to sheep that remain on their own part of the fell where they were born even though it is unfenced –

every year shepherds used to round up strays and take them to Shepherds Meets and Merry Neets held in the autumn. The shepherds would identify their own sheep by their own individual markings to ears and pop marks. Merry Neets started as a 'do' after the annual sheep swapping (Shepherds Meet), usually held at a pub for a meal and a drink, and followed by story telling and songs. Two of the best known were held regularly at Mardale and Troutbeck.

Fun and games on Smithy Brow. I remember in the early 1940s about the time this photograph was taken of doing just the same as the children are doing here, taking my homemade wooden sledge onto Chapel Hill and sledging down to Smithy Brow at great speed. We always had someone keeping a watch at the bottom, in case the local policeman caught us as we would be in for a telling off!

My school hockey team photograph from the 1950s with Mrs Watson, a school teacher. In the top row are Anna Woodburn, Lilly Adams, Judy Black. Middle row: Kathryn Stainton, Rose (author), Edna Barton, Mrs Watson. Front row; two from St Anne's Home   ?   ; Anne Hall;   ?   home; Pat Greenhow. St Anne's Home Girls invariably wore gym slips.

Ambleside Amateur Boxing Club

There has been some kind of boxing club in Ambleside since the late 1800s. We know that Fred Armer first used a small room behind Harold Ashburner's repair shop, in St Mary's Lane as a boxing room in the 1930s. Fred Armer, a shoemaker who worked at Tyson's shoe shop, was the trainer. They moved to the YMCA in St Anne's Road but this was too big so they rented the Drill Hall at The Green and paid 2/6 (12½p) per week (each boy paid 3d). One of their first games was against the Windermere Club and their prize was a pair of second-hand boxing gloves each. They later moved to cheaper premises, renting an old garage behind the Royal Oak Hotel for 1/6 (7½ p) per week from Mr Guy Thompson, owner of the Wines and Spirits' shop.

Mr Thompson was so pleased with them for doing up the premises that he let them use the garage rent-free for six months. The building was so small that they only had ropes on two sides of the ring and the two walls were padded with straw mattresses. The punch bag was an old army kit bag and was filled with old clothes. The area was so small that half the boxers used to have to go for a six-mile run while the others boxed or waited their turn. They had contests all over Cumberland. They were not affiliated to the Amatuer Boxing Association and called themselves the Ambleside Boys' Boxing and Physical Culture Club, wearing black and amber shorts (orange waistband and stripe down the side).

Ambleside Boys' Boxing and Physical Culture Club in their premises behind the Royal Oak in c.1930, phographed by R S Sanderson of Grasmere.
Back, left to right: Jackie Strickland, Les Hodgson, Ashton Sproat, Tommy Garside,   ?.
Middle, left to right: Ernie Stubbs, Johnnie Hodgson, Bill Sproat, Sam Garside, Frank Bell.
Front, left to right: Norman Garside,?   , Meakin, Les Stephenson. Fred Armer their trainer.   *(Photo: Sam Garside)*

Tournaments were held at the Queens Pavillion, in the Queens Hotel. Benson, the blacksmith, provided the iron to make the ring and Lennie Anderson, a joiner, did a lot of the work and Alf Hayton was promotor. It proved very successful.

The next notable spell of boxing came in 1949, after the war and the club was back to using the YMCA. They had some good boxers, Peter, Dennis and Ian Irwin, Kenny Thornborough, Johnny, Tony and Dave Routledge, Geoff Smith, Terry and Ronnie Middleton, Martin and Dennis Phillipson, Dave Morton and Dave Reynolds. There was thirty boys in the club then and out of these seven or eight would travel round the country to tournaments. Dr Lancaster did all the medicals free of charge and covered at ringside. The club was now affiliated and had the strongest team in the northwest of England and travelled to Liverpool (noted for its players and fights) and Manchester.

The lads boxed well – notably Tony Routledge was the first person to get through to the Northern Counties and Junior ABA Chaionshionship for the United Kingdom Finals. Ian Irwin is now an English National Coach. Dave Reynolds is a timekeeper and judge who sits on the English panel of judges, referees and supervises at championships as well as acting as adjudicator. The club has undoubtedly had outstanding success for such a small town.

The club moved once again in 1970 to a barn at the Golden Rule and now has both girls and boys in the club, with Dave Reynolds as their trainer.

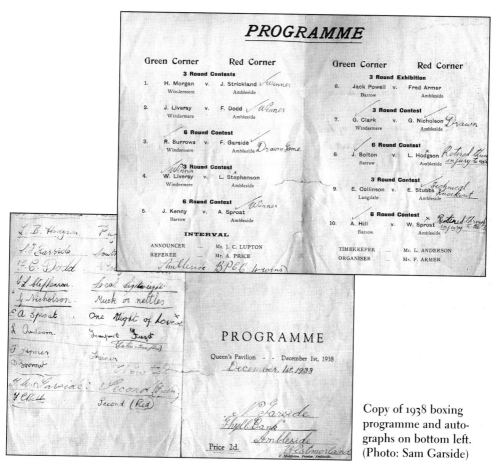

Copy of 1938 boxing programme and autographs on bottom left. (Photo: Sam Garside)

Two personal wartime photographs. Above shows my mother and father, with me on the left and with my sister, Irene on the right. Below, our family increased when the evacuees arrived in Ambleside - we had the Moore family from Newcastle-upon-Tyne who are photographed here. Front left is Duncan, Billy, Irene, and Charlie with their mother standing behind.

Note: Ambleside families had two large groups of evacuees sent from Newcastle to stay with them, in 1939 and in 1940. In 1940 the 'Dame Allen Girls School' complete with all the staff moved and they shared the Kelsick School. The locals attended in the morning and the Dame Allen Girls had the school in the afternoon.

CHAPTER FOUR

LAKE ROAD (NORTH)

This photograph by Herbert Bell shows horse manure in plenty outside Walton's Confectioners shop in Lake Road. On the right is the old Stamp House (Tax Office) which supported the Wordsworth family for many years in the early nineteenth century, when William Wordsworth was Distributor of Stamps for the County of Westmorland from March 1813 to July 1843. (There is now a plaque proudly displayed next to the door of building for all to see). The stamp tax was levied on legal documents – for which he received an annual remuneration.

Herbert Bell (1856 – 1946)

The Ambleside chemist and local well renowned photographer, was one of three sons and six daughters of Thomas Bell, an Ambleside Chemist, whose business was in Lake Road, Ambleside (Bell's the Chemist is still here today), and they lived above the shop. Herbert had a good education and attended Eller How School, run by a Miss Clough, sister of the poet Arthur Hugh Clough.

On leaving school Herbert was apprenticed to his father and his route to photography was through chemistry. He began his portrait practice in the mid 1870s and this provided him with an income before becoming a landscape photographer.

In the 1880s he went with his brothers and a group of friends into the fells with tents and camping equipment (the tent doubled as a dark room). He started getting away from the formal group photography and many of his informal photographs also show him in the shot – taking advantage of delayed action cameras.

Importantly he also made many studies of working people in the Lake District – photographing slate quarry workers, bark peelers and shepherds – giving us a precious permanent record. He married in 1887 and acquired Strawberry Bank, an old farmhouse on the lower slopes of Wansfell and had two daughters.

Between 1894-1907 he did a photographic survey of Westmorland's historic buildings. He was so well thought of that he was commissioned on John Ruskin's death in 1900 to photograph all his drawings and watercolours.

In 1906 he compiled a photograph book of Ambleside and neighbourhood by early nineteenth century artists in which William Green predominates.

He used to say that he had taken his first walk on Scafell when he was ten years old and his last when he reached eighty!

He had many well-to-do friends and was a highly respected figure in Lake District society. He was one of the founder members of the Armitt Library where it is only fitting that his large collection of quality photographs and equipment are kept today and to which Ambleside is indebted.

Further south along Lake Road, we have Banks Stationers, Tobacconist and Newsagents, in this turn of the nineteenth/twentieth century picture. On the left is the business of Herbert Bell, the famous Ambleside photographer, most of whose archive is to be seen in the town's Armitt Library along with his early equipment.

The following views are from different times during the early twentieth century in Lake Road, Ambleside. On the left is Mashiter's grocers shop and just beyond is Slater's Private Hotel. Opposite on the right is the building that housed the Armitt Library for many years before moving to rooms over the Public Library.   *(Photo: G P Abraham of Keswick)*

The fine open tourer motor car, with its solid spokes and rubber tyres, is seen picking up guests from Hill's Waverley Hotel and the porter is poised ready to open the door. This hotel was previously owned by Slater's and in my day it was 'The Vale View' and today it is called, 'Churchills'. Note the modernised front to the hotel. The ladies are smartly dressed in 1920s dress attire and the men are in plus fours. On the right of the picture just showing is a gas street lamp.

The alleyway just to the left where the car is parked, leads to the local cobbler, Cecil 'Tickle' Otway – who is still working today in his 90s!   *(Photo: Octavius C Wilmot of Ambleside)*

An early motor bus has just passed Hill's Private Hotel on its way to Windermere. On the right can be seen Atkinsons Country Stores and Viponts Café (now called 'Pippins'). My mother who was a very good cook, always bought gingerbread and parkin as a treat for us from here.

(Photo by G. P. Abraham of Keswick)

A rare view of an Ambleside policeman (probably the Sergeant) complete with helmet and tap stick from the 1920s, standing outside the White Lion Hotel with the Royal Oak Hotel on the left, then run by the Jackson family. Note the tap stick was used to communicate with other officers by tapping it on the pavement through the night. The sound would travel loud and clear through the silent streets.

Competition outside the White Lion Hotel. This picture by O F Stengel of London shows four very worn out horses with their coach, whilst some passengers appear to be dismounted admiring a passing motor charabanc. A replacement horse can be seen on the right being brought down from Taylor's stables, which was located next to the Salutation Hotel.

E 38659

Photograph of 'Tickle' Otway busy at work in the 1970s.

(Photo: Paul Allonby)

'Tickle' in 2001 working in his shop.
(Photo: Anne Bonney)

Cecil Gibson Otway

Known to all as 'Tickle' Otway this ninety year old is still carrying on his business repairing shoes from his converted garage in Stamp House Yard, just off Lake Road. This book would be incomplete without a mention of this remarkable man. I asked, "How did you get the name Tickle?" "If you were given Cecil as a Christian name, you were automatically called 'Tickle,' in my day and the name has always stuck," was his reply.

He left school at fourteen to work at Stables, the shoemakers in Church Street, Ambleside (later it moved to Lake Road and is now the Beatrix Potter shop). Tickle served his apprenticeship there. He started work at the bottom and worked long hours for very little pay. Then, they made all the thread, from hemp and used their own specially prepared wax. This was made from a mixture of pitch and oil (or mutton fat). The ball or stick wax was then put on the leather and ironed with a warm iron to give it a good polish. Tickle was given the job of sticking patches on, then progressed to attaching the uppers and finally learning the craft of putting together the whole boot or shoe, by the time he was nineteen.

Tickle used to deliver the shoes after closing time by bike. Four people worked at the shop at this time – Jonathan Stables, Mr Harris (his brother-in-law), Harry Dugdale and Tickle (sometimes they had a traveller). He remembers getting 4/- (20p) per week to start with and one week unpaid holiday a year.

When he had completed his apprenticeship at twenty-one, sadly for him they dispensed with his services. He then worked for a short time for his father before being taken on at Horrax's Bobbin Mill at the bottom of Stock Ghyll. He was soon to be 'jack of all trades' there and enjoyed his work. A duodenal ulcer prevented him from 'joining up' during the war, so he carried on working at the Bobbin Mill. During the war they carried out war work, making bobbins for wiring in aeroplanes, parachute silk, as well as making games, draughts and suchlike.

Whilst working at Horrax's he received a bad stomach injury from which he almost died. He turned again to his former trade and in 1944 he rented a wooden shed for 2/6 (12½p) a week in Stamp House Yard, from which he has never looked back. He still proudly has to this day, the notebooks where he meticulously kept his customers' foot measurements, of the shoes and boots he has made. His best customers were the farmers and quarrymen but he has handmade shoes for the gentry, evacuees who stayed during the war in Ambleside, Charlotte Mason students and for early fell walkers. Tickle always commences making his shoes two sizes bigger than what the finished article should be.

Tickle proudly drove the first motorised ambulance and made many journeys to Kendal in his forty-three years. Among his proudest possessions is the BEM he received from the Queen and equally so, a book signed by many of the residents of Ambleside thanking him for his work with the ambulance and mountain rescue service during these years.

He built two shops for himself, meaning one for selling shoes and the other for repair, but today they form the Ambleside branch of the Cumberland Building Society. His business today is in the converted garage at the rear and he lives above, overlooking the town and people he loves. He has a smile and friendly word for everyone. He often receives mail from overseas, from people he has befriended during their stay in Ambleside and on their return home, have sat down and written thanking him for his friendship whilst they were here – they are the lucky ones to have found Tickle and his premises tucked away down Stamp House Yard.

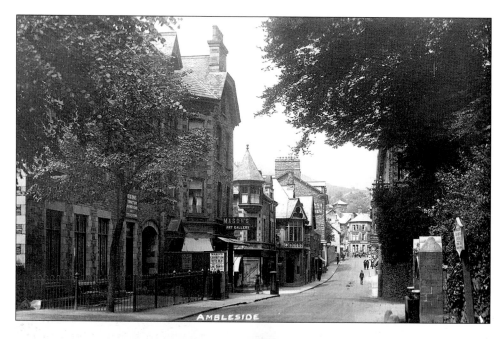

Above: On the left is 'Mason's Corner' on Lake Road, which took its name from the art gallery which can be seen second on the left. Dixon's Furniture Showroom and Storeroom can also be seen here on the left. Note the fountain on the right with provision for refreshments for both human and horses, like the trees it is sadly now gone.

Left: The Smallwood Hotel in Compston Road, in the heart of Ambleside in the 1930s. A young lady and girl in white starched aprons are standing proudly outside. The building was originally built by a family of stonemasons called Smallwood. The iron railings were removed during World War Two for scrap iron to help with the war effort. I remember standing at school watching workmen with acetylene torches removing them all.

CHAPTER FIVE

MARKET PLACE, CHURCH STREET AND ST MARY'S CHURCH

At the top of Church Street is the Royal Oak Hotel seen above in a Stengel photograph in about 1902, when the Lamb family, were the proprietors. Note the two ladies walking on the left of the photograph with long full length dresses/skirts, coats and hats and a lady at the front door of the hotel (possibly the proprietress), dressed in long skirt and white blouse.

Church Street is seen here in a 1930s view by Atkinson and Pollitt of Kendal, with Loughrigg behind. Motor cars have arrived and Clark & Gibson had cycles for hire. Third on the right – Gatey, Heelis & Son where I first worked as office junior – one of my jobs was the collection of rents. (Mr Heelis was the husband of Beatrix Potter and was a solicitor, with other offices in the area, including Hawkshead).

Asplins & Sons, Butchers, Established 1881, on the left near where the van is parked – had queues every morning for their fresh homemade pies and delicacies.

The sycamore tree, which adorned the middle of this early twentieth century photograph of Church Street for many decades, was sadly sawn down in 1952.

Ambleside centre in this 1870s, photograph, with the Salutation Hotel in the background on the left and on the right the Queens Hotel. The field at the front had already been built on when I was a child and was a bus station (built in 1930). This was later knocked down to build the Market Cross Shopping Centre in 1997. This is an early Payne & Jennings photograph.

(Photo: John Marsh Collection)

A rare turn of the century view of an early motor coach at the then new Ambleside Bus Station, with their office on the left. The passengers wishing to travel on top did so by climbing a wooden ladder as they did in the horse coach days.

Market Place, on a summer's day with the Market Cross in the forefront. The Market Cross has moved location from its original location, on Lake Road at the Market Hall.

Left: Early 1900s photograph by Lowe of Patterdale, of North Road, Ambleside, from the John Marsh Collection. This road continues up to Kirkstone Pass. The Unicorn Public House can be seen on the left and is still here today. On the right midway up, is Cherry Tree Cottage, where Mrs Fisher took in paying lodgers.

Below: A close-up photograph of Cherry Tree Cottage and the proprietress standing with two smartly dressed young ladies.

St Mary's Church was designed and built by Sir George Gilbert Scott in 1854, when St Anne's Church (commonly called the Old Church) was found to be inadequate to cope with the growing needs of the district. The spire is one hundred and eighty feet high and is made entirely of stone and took four years to build. Windows in the church were placed there in memory of Wordsworth and members of his family. The original concept included a Wordsworth family chapel at the end of the north aisle but this was not realised until 1952.

The much admired mural depicting the rushbearing ceremony by Gordon Ransom is on the west wall and was completed in four months in 1944 (a pupil of Dr E. W. Tristram, who was a noted authority on mediaeval wall paintings). The staff of the Royal College of Art were evacuated to Ambleside from London during the Second World War and this was done as a thank you and a lasting memento of their time here in the Lake District. The painting is twenty-six feet long and approximately twelve feet high and has almost sixty-two full sized figures, including portraits of the then vicar and verger.

I was baptized and married in this church so it holds many special memories for me. The second picture is taken by a Valentine's of Dundee.

The boys of Ambleside School pose for this school photograph in about 1905. In those days of slow speed cameras, smiles were not permitted on school photographs, although a number of the boys in this picture managed to smile.   *(Photo: John Marsh Collection)*

Where today modern motor traffic spoils everything this photograph shows Market Place in about 1900 on a beautiful, calm and peaceful day. I can remember similar days in the 1940s when there was no problem crossing the road. On the left can be seen Simpson's grocers shop and upstairs was the Market Hall (part of the Mechanics Institute). Behind the lady with the cycle is the office of Riggs, the famous coaching firm who pioneered stagecoach services throughout the Lake District and elsewhere. Richard Rigg won the Royal Mail contract and his coachmen sported white box hats and red coats with brass buttons. Later tickets for the railway could also be obtained from them. In the background behind the fir trees is the house occupied by Ambleside's famous artist, William Green. Unfortunately, the house was pulled down to be replaced by the new Post Office.

William Green (1760-1823)

William Green was born on 25th August 1760, in Manchester. His father was a teacher and former clerk of the local church. William's mother sadly died eleven days after his birth. William went to mathematical school. He was recommended to William Yates of Liverpool and engaged on his survey of Lancashire. This is the reason why William first came to the Lake District, where he stayed in Ulverston and met Thomas West, whose Guide to the Lakes had just been published. This, undoubtedly, encouraged him to become an artist.

He opened his first school for drawing and painting in 1783 and in 1786 included accounting in Manchester. William came to live in Ambleside in 1800 and William and Dorothy Wordsworth had just arrived the year before and they became good friends.

He was said to be the first Lake District artist to depict the local views and scenes as they really were and not as they thought the scenes should be. Green was an avid worker and was out in all weathers and had two favourite methods of producing prints – soft ground etching and aquatint (greens and blues). It was said that he only sketched the outline with crayon and washed them afterwards with Indian Ink. He exhibited regularly at Ambleside and Keswick, producing prints, paintings, drawings, etchings and engravings. He had many customers both locally and countrywide.

William died on 29th April 1823, leaving a widow, five sons and four daughters and on his headstone in Grasmere churchyard is an epitaph written by his friend, William Wordsworth:

> *Sacred to the memory of William Green,*
> *the last twenty-three years of whose life*
> *was passed, in this neighbourhood where,*
> *by his skill and industry as an artist he*
> *produced faithful representations of the*
> *country and lasting memorials of its more*
> *perishable features.*
> *He was born at Manchester and died at*
> *Ambleside on the 29th day of April 1823*
> *in the 63rd year of his age deeply lament-*
> *ed by a numerous family and universally*
> *respected. His afflicted widow caused this*
> *stone to be erected.*

It was said that Green's work is the proper supplement to Wordsworth's own powerful statements about the special status of the Lake District as a source of National Property! A number of William Green's pictures and prints are in the Armitt Museum.

Photograph of the Market Hall and Clock Tower. This was the Mechanics Institute and the clock is still called the 'Mechanics Clock' today. This building in the 1900s was available to working class men to join for a small fee and this enabled them the use of the billards room, reading room and library where they could borrow books to improve their knowledge and education. The building today houses different businesses, though outwardly it appears the same.

This party are visiting Ambleside from the Prince of Wales Hotel on an open horse-drawn coach with the ancient Ambleside Market Cross on the left. On the back of the coach reads 'Returning by the residences of the late H. Mr W E Forster, Fox Ghyll and Dr Arnold, Fox How. This picture by O F Stengel of London from about 1900 shows on the left the Salutation Hotel, which was then owned by the Taylor family. They also ran an extensive coach and horse business from the building to the right of the Hotel. At one time they were said to have as many as seventy horses and hired them out as a coach and four to visitors.

SALUTATION HOTEL, AMBLESIDE.   *M. BRACKEN*, Proprietor.
(*Late of County Hotel, Kendal*)

An early sketch of the Salutation Hotel around the late 1880s – giving the name of M Bracken the then proprietor, late of the County Hotel, Kendal – this card was sold as an advertisement for the hotel.

Coaches assemble on the forecourt of the Salutation Hotel about the time of the First World War. In the background is Taylor's stable block and tales are still told in Ambleside about the fate of worn out coach horses, who were killed on the side of Stock Beck, which gave the stream its other lesser known and gruesome name of 'Butcher Beck'. Note the advertisements on the billboards and wooden stepladder used by the passengers to enable them to get seated on top of the coach. The building, which was Taylor's stable block, is now a Woollen Mill shop.

Anthony Chapman (1914-1982)

Anthony was a well-known huntsman with the Coniston Foxhounds (founded in 1825). Hunting has been carried on in this area for centuries, partly from necessity for the need to keep down foxes and partly from the love of the sport. Born at Cote Howe Cottage, Rydal, he was the second son of George and Hannah Chapman. Anthony used to help his father with the hunt and then in 1926-32 he became a whipper-in before becoming huntsman in 1944. He became the third generation of huntsman in his family. His grandfather, William Chapman had been a huntsman for the Windermere Harriers.

The hunt season is from September to May. The Coniston pack has fifty-five hounds and they cover an area on foot as far as Grasmere, Langdale, Witherslack and Kentmere. The hounds are housed at Greenbank Kennels, Ambleside during the hunt season. After May they go home for the summer (to rest) and stay with local farmers and families. Anthony retired in 1976 and sadly died in 1982. He was enormously popular with huntsmen and followers alike. He was also a founder member of Ambleside Sports. As an epitaph Bruce Logan (Master of the Coniston Foxhounds 1954-76) wrote:

> *His deeds they will oft be related in song*
> *And though he has gone to that haven of rest*
> *We will cherish his memory as one of the best*

Anthony Chapman, huntsman with the Coniston Foxhounds, seen here on the Mayor's Hunt, at Troutbeck in the 1970s with Tommy Graves in the left of the picture.

(Photo: Paul Allonby)

Indeed, Fred Nevinson in his book 'A Westmorland Shepherd, his life, poems and songs' dedicated a song to his memory called 'A Tribute to Anthony Chapman (1914-1982)

A TRIBUTE TO A HUNTSMAN
(In memory of Anthony Chapman of the Coniston Hounds)

I sing you a song of a Huntsman
A man we all thought so grand
When he hunted the Coniston Foxhounds
He was the best in the land
Round Scandale, Rydal and Grasmere
He hunted with many a friend
And on every rock and hill end.

Chorus
So we'll all bid farewell to our Chappie
No more a hunting he'll go
But as long as we live we'll remember
The sound of his view Tally Ho!

Those Coniston hounds they adored him
In his terriers he took great pride
When he set off to hunt in the morning
Everyone would be at his side
Through all the years we have hunted
Our pleasure it knew no bounds
When we hunted with Anthony Chapman
And his gallant Coniston Hounds.

Chorus

He was one of Lakeland's great Sportsmen
Like those whose songs we have sung
But the songs that we sing about Chappie
Will be in our own Lakeland tongue
He was respected by each one who knew him
And where he'll be now is quite plain
I know I will give a great "Hallo!"
If somewhere I meet him again.

Chorus

Ambleside Rushbearing

The Annual Rushbearing Procession is held on the first Saturday of July. Adults and children of all ages carry bearings covered in moss and decorated with flowers through the streets stopping at Market Place, where the bearings are lifted high for all the people to see and the rushbearing hymn is sung. The procession then proceeds down to the church where a service is conducted and all the bearings are left for everyone to admire. On leaving the church all get a piece of gingerbread made at the local bakeries.

This ancient event marks the custom of taking fresh rushes to lay on the floor of the church, in the days when church floors were bare earth, and was also a thanksgiving and merry-making after the hay crops were safely gathered in.

On the following Monday there is a sports day for the children who entered the rushbearing.

William Wordsworth never missed this occasion and he and his Rydal party would sit in a little room belonging to Agnes Nicholson, the then postmistress of Ambleside. This was an occasion for all to come, take part in and enjoy!

The picture opposite shows the people of Ambleside at the 1908 Rushbearing Celebration a tradition that is still carried on today and watched by tourists and locals alike.

The Ambleside Rushbearers' Hymn was written in 1835 by the Rev. Owen Lloyd (1803-1841), Curate of Ambleside, which has been used ever since. The hymn is sung in the Market Place, where the procession halts for a short time, the music is provided by the Town Band before moving off to make its way to the Parish Church.

Our fathers to the House of God,
As yet a building rude,
Bore offerings from the flowery sod,
And fragrant rushes strew'd.
May we, their children, ne'er forget
The pious lesson given,
But honour still, together met,
The Lord of Earth and Heaven!

Sing we the good Creator's praise
Who sends us sun and showers,
To cheer our hearts with fruitful days,
And deck our world with flowers!
These, of the great Redeemer's grace,
Bright emblems here are seen!
He makes to smile the desert place
With flowers and rushes green.

This shows the 1911 procession, showing many men in straw boaters and the girls beautifully dressed carrying the floral hoops and arrangements.

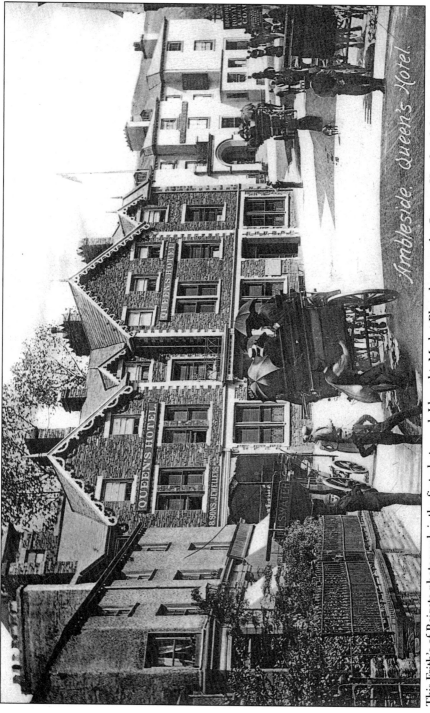

Ambleside. Queen's Hotel.

This Frith's of Reigate photograph is the first photograph I bought. Market Place between the Queens Hotel and the Rigg's Coach Office was where holiday makers joined the turn of the century coach trips which were called 'rounds'. You could get trips to Ullswater and over to Kirkstone; Keswick via Dunmail; Hawkshead and Coniston; and the scenic journey along the side of the Lake to Windermere. A good choice was always available. The people are using umbrellas to shield themselves from the sun.

Ambleside, Market Place.

This Frith's photograph shows how busy Ambleside was in the early 1900s. These Lakeland visitors were wealthy people who had heard about the beauty of the fells and countryside surrounding the Lakes from the romantic artists and poets who came to live here. These people bought land and built mansions and hotels and some even rented. These were some of the people who would have gone on perhaps the Grand Tour of Europe and later when transport improved the rest of the population.

In the mid-nineteenth century Wordsworth had been against an extension of the railway from Windermere to Low Wood or round the shoulder of Wansfell to Ambleside itself. Again, in November 1896 proposals were made and a Bill placed before Parliament – but to no avail. There were the usual arguments for and against, but in the end as usual, it all came down to money. The London and North Western Railway Company refused to back it and the figure was too large an amount to be raised locally. Had a railway been allowed we would probably not have had as many problems as we have today with the motor car.

The empty Market Place outside the Queens Hotel is in sharp contrast to the previous two scenes. Note the coach ladders again outside both the Queens Hotel and Riggs. These were used as mentioned earlier to enable passengers to get onto the top of the coaches.

Below the scene of the Market Cross in the 1930s, includes an MG Sports car. Motor traffic over the next thirty years was to transform this part of Ambleside. Ambleside was granted its Market Charter in 1650 and in 1688 James II granted a similar charter and power to collect tolls for the benefit of the poor. The Market Cross has been moved and re-erected at least twice.

CHAPTER SIX

RYDAL ROAD AND STOCK GHYLL AREA

The most photographed building in the Lakes, the Bridge House, Rydal Road, dates from 1843. It was built as a garden house originally to span Stock Beck, and connecting the gardens of the former Ambleside Hall to the orchard that lay on the other side of the beck. 'Chairy' Rigg a basket maker and chair repairer brought up six children here in the 1850s. In the early 1900s it was noted that there was no water, privy or ash pit.

This photograph was taken by, James Atkinson of Ulverston in about 1902. Today the National Trust owns the building.

This photograph of Rydal Road was taken about 1900 when there was little traffic and the locals could safely stand chatting in the middle of Stock Beck Bridge. I was born in the cottage where the lamp can be seen (in the middle of the picture) – 3 Smithy Brow. In the background can be seen Low Nook as it was in its original form. Low Nook is now the home of the Armitt Library and is part of the Teachers' Training College.

On the right is Tyson's Boot and Shoe Makers shop and later it became a sweet shop owned by May Turner when I was a child. The street to the right was known as Bridge Street, but carried the name of Rattleghyll (the noise from the mills) or in my day 'Bug Alley.'

Armitt Library

The Armitt Library was started in 1912. A plaque inside the Library today in Rydal Road, simply reads:

> Mary Louisa Armitt
> Founder of the Armitt Library and Museum
> Ambleside historian, musicologist and ornithologist
> Lived at Hawkshead 1886-1894 and at Rydal Cottage
> Born in Salford 24th September 1851
> Died at Rydal, 31 July, 1911

The library partly came about through the great wealth of intellectuals and artists that settled in and around Ambleside during the nineteenth and early twentieth centuries and their friends that came and visited them. The list appears endless, William Wordsworth, Dr Arnold, John Ruskin, Harriet Martineau, Matthew Arnold, Hartley Coleridge, Thomas de Quincey, Arthur Ransome, William Purdom (early plant hunter), Charlotte Mason and Beatrix Potter to name but some. Painters, poets, educationalists, authors and historians became subscribing members.

The Armitt, like other libraries, has gone through difficult times and been sited in two other locations in the town before coming here – but is going from strength to strength.

Many of the early members have generously bequeathed books from time to time and helped in its development. There was no county record office when it was formed and it became a natural depository of unusual books, literature and personal effects of some of the famous people who lived in our area. The trust lost its old home in 1973 and moved to above the Library until this present building was built, with various grants in 1997.

Mary L Armitt's instructions were that:- "The aim of the Bequest is not to furnish a free Library for the Town, but to create a Collection of Books of Scientific, Literary or Antiquarian value, which may be made available for the Student and the Book-lover."

The 'Armitt' as it is affectionately named is open daily and now includes a museum which has grown from the library, with exhibits about the life and work of famous people who came and settled here. The library is free 'for the student and book lover' who want to study and learn more about the Lake District and its people.

The Armitt today. (Photo: Anne Bonney)

Rydal Road around 1940, showing Bridge House and opposite Rydal Road Garage owned by Mr Samuel Hunter Ellis.

HOUSE OF EDUCATION, AMBLESIDE.

Fairfield House, Ambleside

What do you think of this?

Above: This picture of the Houses of Education, Ambleside, was taken by Raphael Tuck & Sons. In 1892 Charlotte Mason (1842-1923) the daughter of a Liverpool merchant, opened her 'House of Education', in Rydal Road. Miss Mason, a teacher, came to Ambleside and with a friend formed this teacher-training establishment. Many of her student teachers became governesses. She began correspondence courses. When Green Bank came on the market, the home of Wordsworth's niece, Dorothy (Mrs Benson Harrison) it was purchased and was called Scale Hall, the main college building today. From its small beginnings the college became known as Charlotte Mason College and today is part of St Martin's College, Lancaster and is synonymous with teacher training today.

Left: Fairfield House, Ambleside in the early 1900s taken by Herbert Bell. This house became part of Charlotte Mason College. The students did their practical teaching firstly using village children and then it became a boarding school. This was one of the buildings on Rydal Road the other they used was just known as the Annexe. Today it still houses students.

The forecourt of Garside's Garage and Coach Works was the starting point for the May Queen Float as seen in these turn of the nineteenth/twentieth century photographs. The May Queen Festival was held for many years with the proceeds going to the Westmorland County Hospital in Kendal. The Vicar in the bottom picture can be seen holding a Red Cross collecting box. Note the two advertisements for motor car oil – Vacuum and Sternol.

The Old Mill, Ambleside.

Above: Photographed by Lillywhite's of Yorkshire, this charming view is of Stock Beck (Butcher Beck), alongside Ambleside Mill, the water wheel can be seen on the right.

Left: Stock Ghyll Falls, Ambleside. Stock Ghyll Park was originally the property of the Stock Park Trustees. The River Stock, from which the park takes its name, plunges down a very steep and rocky ravine of some seventy-six feet and is a popular beauty spot. I have many happy memories of the Teasdale family who for many years lived in the cottage at the top end of Stock Ghyll Park. Mr Teasdale looked after the grounds and kept the falls clean and tidy after the many visitors had gone home. This photograph is from about 1905 and is by Brockbank's of Windermere.

THE LATEST
FASHION
at
AMBLESIDE.

The holiday trade in Ambleside catered for all tastes and here can be seen two of the early 'Wish you were here!' cards, which holiday makers loved to buy and send home. These are colour photographs and the lady's hat has been carefully made of fine red velvet and pink ribbon – hand made no less!

There are many Ambleside jokes about courting a lass who lived at the Kirkstone Pass Inn – this of course is the situation reversed!

HER SWEETHEART LIVES AT
AMBLESIDE
AND SHE AT KIRKSTONE PASS
HE HAS TO CLIMB BY AEROPLANE
TO SEE HIS BONNY LASS

A beautiful photograph of Ambleside fire station crew, smartly turned out with their tender and horses in the 1880s. The captain standing on the front right of the fire tender is William Benson (relation to Ian Benson the Blacksmith) (Photo: Ambleside Fire Station)

A photograph taken by Octavius C Wilmot of Ambleside of the Fire Brigade and Committee, proudly posing with a shield they won c.1928 for best turned out Engine Pump.

Back row, left to right: Firemen B Backhouse, G Keen, F Atkinson, Engineers H Hodgson and T Beetham.

Middle row, left to right: Engineer J Dugdale, Firemen J Airey, H Holmes and W Nicholson.

Front row, left to right: Fireman J Fisher; J T Battersby (Gas & Water Manager); G Aitchison Esq (President of NFBA, Chairman of AUDC); Captain T S Huddlestone; Dr Allen (Chairman Gas, Water and Fire Brigade Committee; Lieutenant G Atkinson; G F Yates Esq (Chairman Finance Committee); Firemen W Beetham and W Hindmoor.

(Photo: Ambleside Fire Station)

Ambleside Firemen

Today the fire station is on Rydal Road as you go out of Ambleside. It used to be on Lake Road next to the petrol station (now a Chinese restaurant). The firecrew are highly trained local men who are on 24 hour call. There is one Sub-Officer and ten firemen. They are a part-time retained crew, who live and work in the close vicinity of Ambleside and immediately respond to a call-out, when their pagers are triggered from the Fire Station Headquarters in Cockermouth. They are aged between eighteen and fifty-five and train every Wednesday evening for two hours, besides attending courses and various training sessions. They attended one hundred and sixty call-outs in the year 2000. They are a vital dedicated part of the Ambleside community who couldn't be managed without.

Ambleside Firemen with their fire engine during a training session, pumping water out of the river in the 1940s. Left to right: Baden Ashburne, Jack Huddleston and Jack Atkinson.

(Photo: Ambleside Fire Station)

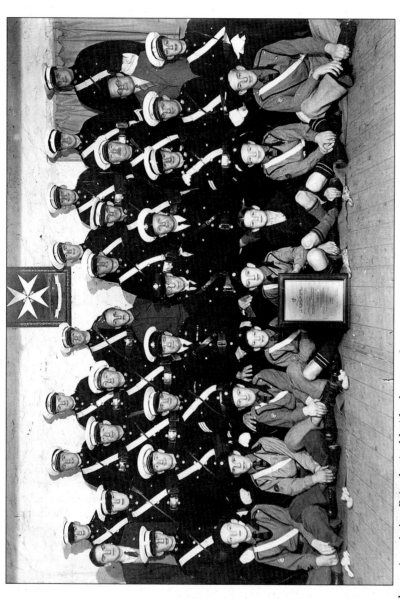

(Photo: John Prickett)

St John's Ambulance Association Brigade, Ambleside about 1936
Back row, left to right: T Stephenson, B Dixon, A Gowling, D Stephenson, ?, W Anderson, ?, ?, ?
Third row, left to right: L Chapman, T Dixon, F Lace, E Atkinson, L Thornbourgh, J Otway, G Whitam, ?, J Hodgson.
Second row, left to right: B Lawson, C Otway, W Frost, A Armstrong, C Taber, G Majer, T Alexander, ?.
Front row, left to right: D Dawson, N Connely, ? Garside, F Dawson, E Garside, ?, T Woodburn and B Prickett

St John's Ambulance Brigade Division, Ambleside

Early records show that there was a St John Ambulance Association Centre founded in Ambleside in 1880. The St John's Ambulance Brigade Division was founded on 16th July 1908 and was based at Ambleside Mission Room, Vicarage Road, Ambleside in 1908 and the Superintendent was W Hogg of Woodroyd, Ambleside. There were twenty-two members – two officers, two corporals and seventeen privates. In 1920 the Divisional Surgeon, Dr Allen (founder member), took over as acting Superintendent and in 1921 the post of Divisional Superintendent was taken over by Cecil Tabor (founder member) until he retired in 1934. Ambleside Division was regularly involved in mountain rescue work during the 1930s.

In 1970s they got their own Headquarters on Stock Ghyll Road. They have eighteen St John's Ambulance volunteers who train regularly every Monday evening. The Division is still going strong today and they attend sports events, sheep dog trials, Carlisle Race Course and Records Week on Windermere – just as we have always done

Peggy Hill is situated in the centre of Ambleside. The building to the right and just out of sight, was the local fish and chip shop, once run by David and Irene Woodhouse (my sister and her husband) in the early 1960s. Anybody the worse for drink was not allowed to go up the steep narrow stairs to the small dining area for obvious reasons. The famous sculptress, Josefina de Vasconcellos lived in Wash House Cottage, opposite the chip shop for many years before she moved.

Josefina de Vasconcellos

(Photo: Bernard Kunicki)

Josefina de Vasconcellos

Born in 1904 and only child of a wealthy Brazilian Diplomat is one of our most eminent living sculptors. She remembers her interest in sculpture originating from moulding a birds nest out of the grey mud in the garden at the age of three. A lot of her early education was spent in the New Forest where her Governesses taught her outside, then she went to a convent in Southampton. At fourteen, she set sail to Rio de Janeiro for a year's specialist training. She won a scholarship in 1921 to the Royal Academy. Her stone carving was so expressive that she won runner-up in the 1930 Prix de Rome contest.

At nineteen years of age she was accepted into the Grand Chaumiere in Paris and studied under Bourdelle, one of Rodin's assistants. In 1930 she met the artist and Anglican lay priest, Delmar Bonner, whom she later married. Her father was an atheist and left it for Josefina to decide her religion, thus she was baptised and became an Anglican.

Delma and Josefina adoped two boys and came to the Lake District and settled firstly, in a farmhouse at 'The Bield' in Little Langdale. She worked in an outhouse, whilst Delmar painted on the fells his dramatic landscapes.

From here she later stayed for a while at Isel Hall in 1988 before settling in a small cottage in Peggy Hill, Ambleside. She was also awarded the MBE for her work with disadvantaged children.

There is a long list of her work in 'Who's Who'. A lot of her sculptures are large and she is noted for her free-flowing naturalistic carving. Her work can be seen in many locations, Cathedrals and churches. Locally you can see her work at St Mary's Church, Ambleside - 'In him was life'; Rydal Hall Gardens - 'Escape to Light' and in the Holy Trinity Church, Kendal - 'The family of man'. Some of Josefina's work is also displayed at the Regeneration Gallery in Cockermouth. We are fortunate to have such a great artist living in our midst.

'The Weight of our Sins'
This piece depicts a ten foot derelict cross, being borne by six children, each symbolising a crime against children in the world today.

St Anne's Home for orphan children in 1911 but officially entitled 'Home of St Anne's'

In 1906 this was opened to provide accommodation for eighteen little girls who, through no fault of their own, were homeless or destitute. The young girls would attend church school and the older ones would train as domestic servants. The Church of England Waifs and Strays Society ran the home. Today the school is divided into private houses.

Ambleside Cricket Club

One of the earliest clubs in Ambleside was formed in 1875 and played on White Platts Recreation Ground. They moved to their Rydal ground where they are now in about 1900, renting it from Rydal Hall who had originally laid out the cricket ground. The ground was originally shared with Ambleside Croquet Club who had three or four separate greens. There had also previously been tennis courts there. Twenty five years ago, all the Cricket Club had was a wooden hut but now they have an excellent pavilion, changing rooms, showers and bar facilities.

Ambleside play in the Westmorland Cricket League of which there are five divisions and they have two senior teams. The season runs from the end of April until mid September. They have a strong junior team, players aged between ten and twelve years old and the senior team aged from eighteen upwards. The team practice on Tuesday and Thursday evenings and play matches at weekends round the district and as far a field as Ingleton, Farleton and Morecambe.

The members are drawn from locals, students and seasonal workers. The grounds are still shared during the week, with both Rydal WI and the Senior Citizens using the croquet lawns. It is a beautiful summer pastime, held in surely one of the most picturesque grounds in the country.

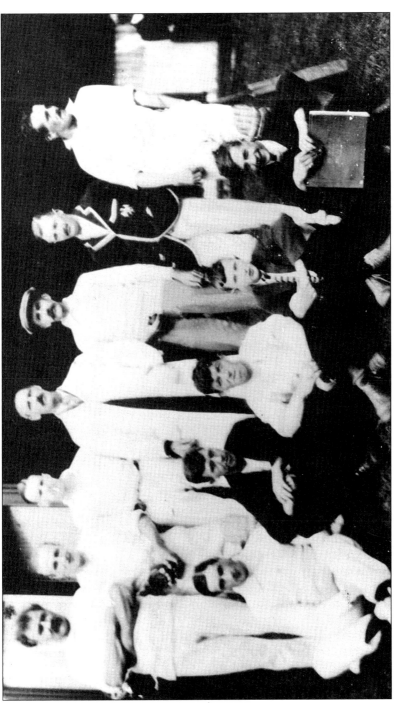

Ambleside Cricket Club pictured here in the Summer of 1919. Back row, left to right:- Cockle Robinson (Verger at St Mary's); Fred Milligan (was first to score a century for Ambleside in the early 1900s);   ?   ; Bill Vity, Sam Alvey (gardener at Ashleigh Green);   ?   ; Harry Rogerson. Front row, left to right: Jim Benson (clerk at Aitchison and Porter Estate Agents, Church St.);   ?   ; Sam German (painter); Harry Wearing and Arnold Graham. (last two names also appear again in Rugby Team!)

(Photo: Ambleside Cricket Club)

Harriet Martineau

(Photo: Kendal Library, Cumbria County Council)

Harriet Martineau (1802-1876)

Born in Norwich of Unitarian parents. She had three brothers and two sisters who were all well educated. The boys went to University and as was the custom in those days, the girls were expected to stay at home, but Harriet had other ideas. In 1823 she had an article on female education published anonymously in a monthly Unitarian magazine. Her brother, James praised the article and when he realised it was Harriet's, encouraged her to write more.

This was the start of Harriet's writing career. She was to write many articles on both women and politics, as well as books on religion and her passion for social reform. She travelled to America where she spent two years.

She moved to the Lake District in the 1840s, bought a plot of land in Ambleside (advised by William Wordsworth) and built a house called 'The Knoll'. In 1852 she joined the staff of the Daily News and over the next sixteen years wrote over sixteen hundred articles. She wrote strongly about the employment of women, education for girls, women entering the medical profession and the granting of the vote. She was a strong and forthright woman who stood up for what she thought. Perhaps her most read work was her novel 'Deerbrook'.

Harriet unfortunately suffered a lot from poor health all her life. She continued to write pamphlets and articles on women's rights until her death from bronchitis, in 1876.

'The Knoll', Ambleside, taken by Abraham's of Keswick.

(Photo: John Marsh Collection)

Two early photographs from the John Marsh Collection. Above shows the officers and assistants of the Ambleside Sports in the early twentieth century. Ambleside Sports first came into being in 1862, Queen Victoria's Golden Jubilee year. They are amateur Lake District Sports, where adults and children take part in running, fell and sprint races, Cumberland and Westmorland Wrestling and hound trailing. This is held in August every year and is still popular today and is looked forward to both by competitors and onlookers alike. The top photo shows the officials and helpers about 1910 and below the commencement of the hound trail. This event is held on the Thursday nearest the 1st August every year and this date can even fall at the end of July.

CHAPTER SEVEN

MILLANS PARK AREA

Ambleside's Wesleyan Chapel is situated in Millans Park and was opened on Whit Monday 1899. It is faced with local dressed stone. There is a memorial window in tribute to the memory of William and David Creighton whose names are associated with the beginnings in 1842 of Methodism in Ambleside.

Ambleside RUFC 1920-21
Back row, left to right: Walter Bennett, Bernard Backhouse, Jack Fisher, Frank Dixon, Sam Hunt and Tosser Robinson.
Middle row, left to right: Des Hawksworth, Ian Tyson and Tom Beetham
Front row, left to right: Geoff Hawksworth, Lance Hawksworth, Eog Bennett, George Whittam, Arnold Graham and Harry Wearing.

(Photo: Ambleside RUFC)

Ambleside Rugby Club

In 1871 Ambleside was the home to many wealthy Lancashire industrialists who introduced the sport to the town. After a few friendly games a club was officially formed in 1874. Over the years the club has met with great success, playing both home and away games. For these early matches the home team came already changed, whilst the visitors had the use of a hut or could change behind the nearest hedge. A second XV was formed and played its first game in 1877. A noted player was F. S. Strickland, known throughout the rugby world as 'The Great Northern Kick' – due to his ability to kick a ball the length of the pitch! In 1884 Ambleside Swifts were incorporated into the team. In 1898 the club decided to sample the game under 'Northern Rules' but in 1902 gave their allegiance to the 'Amateur Code, and on 30th April 1920 the club became Ambleside RUFC.

On 10th May the club got its first permanent home at Kelsick Field. Two beer barrels were purchased for washing purposes after the game! In 1937 the team moved to Rothay Park. No matches were played during the war and the club was reformed in 1947. In 1954 the club was disbanded again, due to a shortage of men as a result of them being 'called-up' for National Service. The club was reformed again in 1960 and in 1966 negotiations began for land at Galava Park, which is now their home ground together with clubhouse and facilities. The 1997-98 has been the club's greatest since its formation. The club captain, Neil Irwin, shattered all records with 238 points to his credit, whilst Mark Shepherd was the leading try scorer with 20 tries. The club and grounds form an important part of Ambleside life and many families have played down the generations. They generously give of their time to train interested youngsters. The club house is used regularly by other Ambleside groups and the grounds too, for such events as the flower show. The Mountain Rescue Team also use the pitch regularly for landing the RAF helicopter in their frequent call-outs.

The rugby match with Greengarth had to be cancelled when this rescue helicopter had landed due to engine trouble on 10th February 2001

(Photo: Anne Bonney)

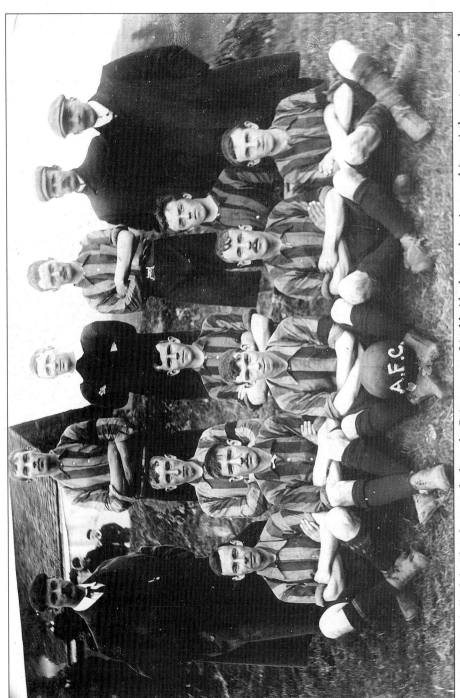

Ambleside Football Club. The photograph above, by R Armstrong of Ambleside shows a late nineteenth/twentieth century team when the stripes on the jerseys were vertical.

Ambleside Football Club

This was formed in 1896 here in Miller Field and they had their first game against the local Rugby Club. The amateur team used to use the cellar of Rotha Jackson's bakery, in Church Street, to change in. They later used the YMCA and in 1980 the Junior School, next to St Mary's Church. Instead of renting it was decided to purchase the field in 1980 from Kathleen Doherty. In the 1990s through generous local donations, the club was able to complete the club house (on 4th August 1995), which was opened by Mrs Ada Hillard and Mr Graham Kelly (Chief Executive of the Football Association). Ambleside United Football Club grounds are called Hillard Park as a mark of respect for their kind beneficiary and friend. The club colours today are blue and white horizontal stripes and they now even have a women's team!

Above can be seen Ambleside Town Team, in 1949 the winners of the High Sherrifs Cup, when the stripes on the jerseys were horizontal green and white strips.

Back row, left to right: Jack Milligan, Les Stephenson, P Wilson, H (Chick) Hardy, Ted Flitters, Bert Hardy and Alf Nevinson (Chairman of Football Club)

Front row, left to right: Peter Wills, Roland Stephenson, Bert Harrison, Harry Shuttleworth, Les Hodgson and Morris Hardy

The corner shop situated at the top of Compston Road and Millans Park, which now houses an outdoor pursuits shop. In the early twentieth century this was the busy ironmongers business of Taylor and Bispham, who also advertised cycles for sale and repair, as well as stabling as part of their business. I remember taking wet batteries here for charging in the early days of wireless sets (radio). This was done weekly, you dropped one off and picked a recharged one up in its place.

Ambleside Post Office on the corner of Vicarage Road and Millans Park used to be sited opposite where Zeffirellis is today (previously the old cinema). This photograph by Brittain & Wright of Stockton-on-Tees from about 1902 shows the building as a Post Office with an interesting array of eight telegraph insulator pots above the front door, as the local telephone exchange was above the Post Office. When the Post Office moved into the Main Street in the mid 1960s, this building became a shop and is now one of the village's fish and chip shops.

CHAPTER EIGHT
KIRKSTONE PASS

An assortment of traffic can be seen on this Pettitt's of Keswick photograph outside the popular 'Kirkstone Pass House' as it was then called, now simply known as the Kirkstone Pass Inn. Motor charabancs are mixed with horse and carriages in that period about 1910, when both ran together for a short time. This popular stopping off point - allow the horses to rest and engines to cool after the slow climb up Kirkstone Pass. People used to have to walk up the hill following the horse-drawn coaches so they were certainly in need of refreshments and rest! Today we have no such hardship!

Early twentieth century advertising for the Kirkstone Pass Inn, some of which is untrue. Arguments in the early twentieth century were long and many about which was the highest inn or inhabited house in England. A number of establishments claimed this honour and still do today!

A view of the narrow road from Ambleside up 'The Struggle' to the Kirkstone Pass Inn - a 'ladies day out' captured by this Abraham's of Keswick photograph. Note also the telegraph poles, which brought modern communication to the Inn.

Sankey's photograph captures the Inn in winter and one of the locals on horseback and shows what conditions can be like. These conditions are still as familiar today and the road is often one of the first to be closed as a result of wintry conditions. Note the old RAC sign hanging outside.

The popular 'Kirk Stone'. From Ambleside this stone is on the left as you go over the summit. It derives this name from its shape – looking like a 'Church' – from a certain angle.

This photograph of the Struggle in 1998 shows the charity 'car pull' that now takes place every year around the end of August. Fourteen men pull a car (weighing one ton) from the Market Cross, Ambleside up the Struggle to the Kirkstone Pass Inn (just a little over 3 miles and 1500 feet above sea level). It first started in 1982 and it then took one hour and twenty minutes. In 2000 it took them just fifty-one minutes and twenty seconds. There is usually a women's team of thirty females and they pull a car (weighing twelve hundredweight). It took them one hour and six minutes to complete the course in 2000.   *(Photo: Dave Reynolds)*

A popular walk from Ambleside was to Sweden Bridge, which can be seen in this early twentieth century photograph by Valentine's of Dundee. This ancient packhorse bridge featured in many holiday photographs is sign posted for all to see off the Kirkstone Pass Road.

CHAPTER NINE

ROTHAY, LOUGHRIGG, CLAPPERSGATE AND SKELWITH

Rothay Bridge pictured here in the 1920s in this delightful photograph by Lilywhite's of Yorkshire. The road over the bridge to the left is to Hawkshead and Coniston. On the right of the picture we have the Rothay Garth Hotel.

One of Sankeys photographs of Rothay Park, Ambleside. Ladies sitting dressed in summer dresses and hats enjoying the afternoon sun around an empty children's paddling pool.

The Croft Hotel, Ambleside, taken by Jospeh Hardman of Kendal. This was built by a Liverpool sugar importer, James Branckner, on the site of a Lakeland farmhouse of the same name about 1827. It was sold in the 1840s and was subsequently owned by Canon Rawnsley, Vicar of Sawrey, and friend of John Ruskin. The building later became a hotel and was taken over by a Yorkshire College as a Field Centre, before becoming derelict. It has been converted to flats. *(Photo: John Marsh Collection)*

An early photograph of 'Fox How' Dr Arnold of Rugby's House built in 1833. Dr Arnold was the eminent scholar and schoolmaster, headmaster of Rugby School from 1828 until his death in 1842. He did not live to spend his retirement in Ambleside. Dr Arnold is immortalised in 'Tom Brown's Schooldays.' His oldest daughter Jane, married Mr William Edward Forster, the Liberal statesman, educationalist and Minister for Ireland who lived at Fox Ghyll.

A lovely turn of the twentieth century photograph at 'The Scroggs', Loughrigg,. The owners are in 'Sunday best' out in their lovely cottage garden, with their welcoming sign on the fence advertising teas to thirsty walkers. This depicts what was available for early tourists.

Miller Bridge, Under Loughrigg, Ambleside under which the River Rothay passes. The purchasers of this card had a delightful walking holiday on the fells but on the way back from one of their walks Bunty and friend 'were chased by a bull!'

Ellers Farm seen here at the turn of the nineteenth and twentieth century when it was still a farm. It dates from 1849 but the part of the building on the right replaced an earlier farm. This was a working farm until the mid 1960s and like many other properties in the Ambleside area the building has now become holiday homes.

Loughrigg - which stands 1101 feet above Ambleside, is a popular hill walk where beautiful panoramic views of Windermere can be seen. In this photograph we see the Coronation bonfire, which was built at the top of Loughrigg to celebrate the Coronation of King George V in 1910 and was apparently fuelled with oil from the Lake Steamers. The large barrel from which the oil is being transferred into a bucket is clearly labelled 'boat fuel'. The local Boy Scout Troop is in attendance.

Brow Head, Loughrigg. The earliest date we have for this old farm cottage is 1707 - and little has changed today. This early photograph was taken by, Octavius C Wilmot of Ambleside

A rural scene that would captivate and delight the early visitor to the Lake District. Abraham's photographer has captured a clipping time scene in the 1920s.

This photograph by Peacock Plating shows hay-making being done the traditional way, with pitchforks and wooden rakes. I remember the horse standing patiently waiting to pull the hay cart home. The hay will be stored above the shippon in the haylofts or in the hay barns for valuable winter fodder.

The famous Stepping Stones, pictured at Rydal, just outside Ambleside on this early photograph by Rotary. This was one of the routes that Dorothy Wordsworth (William's sister) would take on her journey home from Ambleside to Grasmere and is mentioned by her in her writings. The Stepping Stones are still here today and are to be found near Pelter Bridge.

Clappersgate, pictured here by Matthews of Bradford, is a small hamlet situated a few miles outside Ambleside on the road to Hawkshead and the Langdales. Little has changed over the years.

Skelwith Bridge.   2180

The photograph taken from Skelwith Bridge on the outskirts of Ambleside in the 1920s. Looking ahead today we have the Kirkstone Galleries, where local slate products and refreshments can be purchased. There is also a slate manufacturing business close by. This marks not only the boundary of Ambleside but also is the boundary of Westmorland and Lancashire and the end of my photographic journey with you. I hope you have enjoyed it as much as I have!

ON THE ROTHAY NEAR HEAD OF WINDERMERE

SOURCES OF REFERENCE

Herbert Bell - Lakeland Photographer 1856-1946
CITY OF ABERDEEN ARTS AND RECREATION DIVISION 1993
PUBLISHED AS PART OF FOTOFEIS, THE SCOTTISH INTERNATIONAL FESTIVAL OF PHOTOGRAPHY 1993

The Armitt Story Ambleside
BY EILEEN JAY

Charlotte Mason College
BY J P INMAN

William Green of Ambleside. A Lake District Artist 1760 - 1823
BY M E BIRKETT AND J D G SLOSS

William Green article from Dove Cottage Trust (1st March to 27th May 1985)

The Other Ambleside
BY BARBARA CROSSLEY

From Strength to Strength - A book about Ambleside and its Church

Wordsworth's Lakeland
BY JOHN MARSH AND JOHN GARBUTT

Fenty's Album
BY IRVINE HUNT

Kendal Library

Armitt Library

Ambleside Civic Society

Westmorland Gazette

Cumbria Magazine

Amblesidians and friends who have provided pictures and given generously of their own time for which I am truly indebted.

If you have enjoyed this book you may also enjoy other books
published by Helm Press.

'A Westmorland Shepherd' *His life, poems and songs*

'Elephants On The Line' *Tales of a Cumbrian Railwayman (1947-95)*

'Dear Mr Salvin' *The story of the building of a 19th century Ulverston church*

'All In A Lifetime' *The story of a Dalesman as told to June Fisher*

'Hawkshead Revisited" *A Walk in time through Hawkshead*

'A Century of Heversham and Leasgill' *A walk in time through these old
Westmorland villages*

'An Old Westmorland Garage' *The story behind Crabtree's of Kendal*

Helm Press
10 Abbey Gardens, Natland, Kendal, Cumbria LA9 7SP
Tel: 015395 61321
E-mail: HelmPress@natland.freeserve.co.uk